MW00940717

Contents

Disclaimer

This book was written for the purpose of simply guiding you in the right direction when dealing with police on traffic stops. These are my personal recommendations that I would tell my own children to follow. The content within is strictly for informational purposes only. The stories and information are my opinion only and derive from personal experiences. It is impossible for me to tell you how each individual officer will conduct themselves. Every officer is different and will use their own discretion as to how they handle a particular situation they are facing. There is no guarantee that the suggestions in this book will help you or prevent you from receiving citations or other legal consequences. I am a law enforcement officer and not a licensed attorney. You should always seek professional representation from a licensed attorney anytime you need legal advice.

Acknowledgments

Wesley Wyrick – Mentor

Your unconditional guidance in the making of this book proves to be the reason for your massive success. I wouldn't have had any clue where to begin if it were not for you.

Mike Mullins - Mentor

You've always pushed for me to better myself. You've allowed me to bounce ideas off you and provided your years of experience into making those ideas better. Good, bad, and even off the wall ideas, you have never judged me. You've only encouraged.

Adam Dillon – Consultant

Your outside perspective allowed me to tailor this book for the public to better comprehend and understand. Your ideas and challenging questions helped shape this book.

Sondra Dillon – Inspiration

This book wouldn't be possible without your support and motivation. The confidence you have in me is unbelievably inspiring. This is only the beginning of greater things to come. Everything that I have done, everything that I am, and everything that I will become, is because of YOU.

Introduction

Over the years, I have conducted thousands of traffic stops. I have seen all kinds of different reactions from drivers when they see the blue lights in their rear view mirror. I have heard every excuse you can possibly imagine when encountering the public on traffic stops. I regret not starting a journal at the beginning of my career of all the actions and excuses of drivers. If I would have started that journal, then I could have written quite an entertaining book already.

Law enforcement has been in the spot light a lot over the past several years. There has been a lot of negative media coverage on the actions of officers. I believe this has changed the public's perspective of law enforcement and caused a lot of confusion. In particular, confusion with the new drivers.

I have noticed one thing about the way we license new drivers. Parents will take their kids to empty parking lots and teach their kids how to drive. They practice the nomenclatures of the vehicle, how to operate the vehicle, drive in straight lines, where to place their hands, how to check your mirrors, and the most difficult, how to parallel park. They will go to the DMV or online and buy books on how to pass the written test. I can remember studying for months before my test because getting a license meant freedom to me! When they do pass the written, they actually go with an instructor and prove their ability to operate a vehicle. DMV will check a person's eyes to make sure they can properly see. They test them on basic road laws. They even make them prove themselves in the driver's seat. One thing they don't teach, is what to do when getting pulled over by police. They don't teach them what to really expect from the police. They certainly don't teach them how to respond to the officer!

In this book, you will learn the basics of how to properly respond and handle getting pulled over by the police. A concept that even adults and experienced drivers struggle with daily. It's my hope to educate the reader, based on my experience as a law enforcement officer, on how they can make their experience with law enforcement as smooth and as easy as possible. I want them to be calm and not fear the police. I want the reader to know what to expect from the officer as well as what the officer expects from them. Most importantly, how to keep them and the officer safe during the traffic stop.

Chapter 1

Preparation before getting pulled over

Getting pulled over can be a stressful event. It's perfectly normal to be nervous. I've been in law enforcement for nearly 16 years and still get nervous when a police officer is behind me. The one thing that will help calm your nerves is being prepared with the proper documents that will be required if and when you do get stopped by police. Knowing what the documents look like and having them readily available will make your life as well as the officer's life a lot easier. Before you even get in your vehicle and begin driving, you should have a few things ready before you leave.

Proper Documents

Every officer in West Virginia will require three things when they stop you. Your driver's license, registration, and proof of insurance. Some situations may require other documents like transfer paperwork or temporary registration but for now we are going over the basic information.

Your *registration* should be current by checking the date on the top left corner of the card. This should be the physical address where you are currently residing. This card should also have the owner's signature on the back of it.   A lot of families have multiple vehicle's so I recommend you confirming the registration card does in fact belong to the vehicle you're driving and not one of the other family member's vehicle. State Code reference: 17A-3-16, 17A-3-13, 17A-9-2, 17A-3-18

Your *insurance* card should be current just as the registration. This can be checked by confirming the effective dates and expiration dates along with the accurate vehicle information and VIN. When officers ask for this information, you can provide a paper copy or show the officer by using your phone, which is common. State Code reference:17D-2A-3,17D-2A-4

Your *Driver's License* should be current and valid. You can check the status of your driver's license by going to the West Virginia DMV website and typing in your information. Just like with registration and insurance, you should confirm that your address and other information is accurate and current. If you're 15 to 17 years of age, remember that you have certain license restrictions and you should be familiar with these restrictions before you drive. State Code reference: 17B-2-1, 17B-2-3, 17B-2-9, 17B-2-12, 17B-2-13, 17B-4-3.

Location of Documents

I recommend, with the exception of your driver's license,

placing these documents over the visor in your vehicle, rather than in the glovebox or console. This will be more convenient for you to locate and safer for you and the officer, which we go over in the following chapters. They should be kept in an envelope or document holder that is commonly provided by insurance companies. This will maintain legibility and prevent them from tearing up.

Chapter 2

Blue lights in the rearview mirror

When you first see blue lights in your rearview mirror and hear that siren, your anxiety is more than likely, going to increase. Especially if it's the first time you have ever been stopped. I have stopped thousands of cars throughout my career and the one thing I believe that causes anxiety in new drivers is not knowing what to expect. New drivers knowing what to expect will eliminate a lot of unnecessary stress.

Use Your Blinker

You may be in an area where it isn't safe to pull over and you will have to drive a short distance before you can stop. Turn on your right blinker and begin to slow down to let the officer know that you have no intention of running, you are simply trying to find a place to pull over safely.

Safe Location

Officers typically wait for a safe location to where the driver has plenty of options to pull off easily. Sometimes it's difficult and there simply isn't any room on the side of the road, so the officer will go ahead and stop you in the road. It could be a rural area where using the road is the safest or only option.

When possible, find a safe location to pull over so you and the officer are safe. If you pull into a driveway, make sure you pull in far enough to where the officer can also fit his vehicle in behind you and safely line up straight.

Exaggerated Movements

While you are pulling over, the officer is already making observations of you, your actions, and your vehicle. Avoid making any exaggerated movements like reaching in the floorboard or glove box while you're pulling over. The first thing that comes to an officer's mind if he observes this, is the driver is hiding contraband or reaching for a weapon. Just remain with your hands on the steering wheel while pulling over. The officer will give you plenty of time to reach for your documents wherever they may be located.

Radio

Once you have safely stopped, turn your radio off so the officer can easily communicate with you. When your stopped along the side of the road, it's sometimes difficult for the officer to hear you with traffic driving by and even worse if your radio is blaring loudly. This can also be very disrespectful.

Dome Light

If it's nighttime, turn your dome lights on so that you can

retrieve your documents and also ease the officer's mind. The most dangerous time for an officer is upon approach of the vehicle he has just stopped. Officers will be on high alert because they simply don't have any clue what they are about to face when they reach the driver's window. Dome lights allow the officer to easily see inside the vehicle and it assists them in knowing you are not a threat.

Windows

Rolling your driver's side window down has the same safety benefits for the officer as the dome lights. It allows the officer to have a clear view of inside the vehicle, especially if you have dark tinted windows. If you have passengers in the backseat, it's also a good idea to roll the back windows down as well.

Vehicle in Park

Put your vehicle in park. There have been several times I have stopped vehicles and during our encounter, the vehicle would begin rolling. This usually occurs when they are digging for their vehicle information and take their foot off the brakes. I almost had my foot ran over before. Officers are trained to look and see if the vehicle is in park because suspect's will often wait for the officer to get close to the window and far enough away from their patrol vehicle, then they take off and flee. It's not uncommon for an officer to request the driver to place the vehicle in park or even turn the vehicle off. Doing this before the officer even gets up to your window is the best practice.

Visible Hands

Place your hands on the wheel and wait for the officer to approach. This will allow the officer to know that you are not a threat. You don't need to worry about getting any information until the officer asks you to do so. The most important thing to do first is to let the officer know you are not a threat in any way. If there are passengers in the vehicle, they should have their hands in plain view and easy to see by the officer. I recommend they keep their hands on their laps or on the headrest of the front seats.

Stay In The Vehicle

Never get out of the vehicle and walk back towards the officer's vehicle. Officers today will take this as a certain level of threat. The officer has no idea what your intentions are and there have been numerous cases and videos that show drivers exiting the vehicle after being pulled over by police, and engaging in a shootout. They've exited the vehicle and attacked officers and exited the vehicle to take off running. As a consequence, these actions have forced law enforcement to be on high alert if they see the driver's side door open. The most important thing to remember when getting stopped, is to remain in the vehicle unless the officer requests you to exit.

Officer's Approach

This is the most crucial moment for you and the officer. It is the first impression that both you and the officer will have of each other. These first actions are crucial in setting the tone for the entire stop. As said before, the most dangerous time for an officer during a traffic stop is in the approach of the vehicle. Officers don't have a clue what to expect when they first encounter occupants of vehicles. These recommendations are there to show the steps officers would like to see that will decrease any chance of a threat to the officer. Now that you have the initial stop recommendations down, you should have confidence in knowing that you have provided the officer with ease of mind upon his approach the best you can.

Chapter 3

Officers Approach

Officers are trained to never become routine. This chapter is difficult to explain exactly how every officer will make their approach on every traffic stop because it simply varies with every situation. If officers always made an approach of every vehicle the same, then that wouldn't make us very good officers. We would be "sitting ducks" to those who wish to do us harm. I can, however, provide you with a basic idea of what to expect. This will hopefully ease your stress as a new driver.

Driver/Passenger Approach

Many factors go into which side of the vehicle officers will approach. Depending on traffic conditions, stop locations, or officer's instincts, either side can be a possibility. Many people have heard about officers touching the back of the vehicle so their fingerprints can be obtained if something goes wrong during the stop. This can be true but officers are also checking to be sure the trunks are shut and the back hatches shut as well. Officers don't want any suspect surprises coming out of those trunks! Officers could take a passenger side approach if there is heavy traffic on the driver's side. There have been several officers hit by passing vehicles. It may just be a tactical advantage to the officer to make a passenger side approach if the driver is expecting the officer to approach their side. Either way, the important thing for you is to know that the officer may be on either side of the vehicle. Just follow the steps in the last chapter and wait for instructions from the officer.

Initial Conversation

After the officer has made an approach and determined it to be safe he will begin his instructions. The officer may give you further instructions such as putting your vehicle in park or turning it off. Most officers will let you know the reason for being stopped. They may ask you a few questions regarding your violation or actions. They will then request you to provide your license, registration, and proof of insurance.

Explain Your Movements

Your information is best placed above the visor but not required. If you have stored your information in the glovebox or console, then let the officer know first before you dig. Advising the officer beforehand will show the officer that you are not a threat. Wait for his permission before your retrieve the documents from these locations. Anytime that you need to reach for something, just let the officer know. Once you have provided the officer with all the required documents, he will return to his patrol vehicle to run your information through his database.

Hands On The Wheel

Officers train to constantly keep an eye on the occupants of the vehicle that they have stopped. One way to put an officer on edge is to be moving around, digging and reaching for things while he is in his patrol vehicle. You should always keep your hands on the steering wheel and not move around a lot. If the officer observes a lot of movement, he may make another approach of your vehicle to see what you're doing and determined whether you're a threat. It's best to just stay still and be patient while the officer finishes and returns.

Officers Return

When the officer is done running your information and decides whether or not to write you a citation, he will return to your vehicle. If the officer has decided to issue you a citation, then he will explain the requirements. This is not the time to argue, get mad, or throw a fit. We will go over this in another chapter. Your only responsibility at this point is to understand the requirements of the citation and receive a copy. When the officer is done with his instructions, you are free to leave. Officers will say different things to indicate they are done. Things like; "you are free to leave," "Drive careful," "Be careful pulling back into traffic," or "have a good day." When officers say, "have a good day," after you have just received a citation, it is not a sarcastic remark or intentional disrespect. Once you know you are free to leave, then be sure traffic is clear before leaving the side of the road so you don't cause a vehicle crash. Most officers will wait behind you and block traffic so that you can proceed into the lane safely.

Checkpoints

Anytime you make approach of any type of checkpoint, just follow these same directions as if you are being pulled over by the police. The only difference is that you will have a lot of police officers around. They will direct you where to go and what to do.

Chapter 4

Investigative Stops

Sometimes you may encounter officers pulling you over for investigative reasons. When they do, officers will conduct the stop in a different manner. Most of the time, officers will conduct their traffic stops in the previously stated manner but on occasion they may change it up. When they do, just remember to do exactly as they say at the time and later you can figure out why they have done what they did.

Step out of the Vehicle

Law enforcement officers are authorized, when necessary, to require you to step out of the vehicle. This can be for officer safety reasons. An officer may do this when they feel it is safer because of passing traffic. They may ask you to step to the rear of the vehicle so they aren't against the roadside between moving traffic and your vehicle. They may also do this during an investigation if you have passengers in the vehicle. They will remove you as the driver from the vehicle and leave the passengers inside. This will allow them to ask questions and also be at a tactical advantage against the number of occupants in the vehicle. They can also remove you from the vehicle if they suspect you have been drinking. By making you exit the vehicle, they are able to determine whether or not you are intoxicated, stumbling while exiting and swaying while standing. You will see on a lot of social media videos how drivers of vehicles will refuse to step out of the vehicle and argue with the officers on the side of the road. Do not do this in West Virginia. This will result in you potentially being charged with a crime and your vehicle impounded. If you expect this ahead of time, then you will know and understand what the officer is doing. Just know that you will be on your way shortly.

Felony Stops

You're probably thinking, why would I ever be stopped for a felony? This may happen with good reason and you be completely innocent. Officers conduct, what they call "Felony Stops," on persons of high risk, stolen vehicles, and suspects involved in major crimes. As a new driver, you should be aware of this so you can understand that it could happen to you and what to expect if it does. This has occurred in the past on innocent people and for justifiable reasons. For example, officers just received a robbery call that just occurred at a local convenient store. You happen to be driving near the store at the time an officer is responding to that call. The vehicle is described to be the exact vehicle you are driving with no description of a license plate number. You don't have a clue of what just happened but now you're getting pulled over. On felony stops, there will be multiple patrol vehicles behind you. They will have their firearms drawn and pointing at your vehicle. They will order you to turn the vehicle off, roll your window down, place the keys on the roof, open the driver's side door and step out. They will order you to walk backwards towards them and usual get down on the ground to be handcuffed. This process will be repeated for your passengers as well. This seems extreme but I include this because this could easily be you and has happened before. Once everything is figured out, you will be explained the reason and then released. My recommendation if this does happen to you, then just cooperate to the fullest extent because these officers are on high alert.

Questioning

We go over your rights in another chapter but for the purposes of informing you of what to expect, we will go over some of the questioning that officers have on traffic stops. Officers have different ways they may conduct questioning during traffic stops. When questioning, officers are not only looking for the answers you give but also the reaction you have to certain questions. Not long ago, I received a complaint on one of the officers for some of the questions he was asking. After the complaint was made, I realized that the officer did nothing wrong. This person simply didn't know the reasoning behind the questions. Once I explained the reasoning, the complainant understood what had happened. The one thing that officers look for in questioning are "holes" in the story. They are looking to see what doesn't make sense. They want to know what doesn't add up.

Some questions to expect will be the usual ones about the violations you made to be stopped. They may ask you if you were aware of the speed limit or if you knew how fast you were going. If it's a violation of registration or inspection sticker, they may ask if there's underlying problems that would prevent you from getting the updated stickers. If you're on your cell phone they may inquire about the reason. If you have passengers, they may ask for their identifications as well.

Then the officers may go into further questioning with you that may make you feel like a criminal. Believe me when I say this, you are definitely not the only person they have asked these questions. Officers will ask these questions quite often, with or without reason, just to simply hear and see the response that the driver gives. They will ask where are you going? Where are you coming from? The reason is they are simply asking to determine whether it matches the location you are now. They may see if it matches what your passengers are saying.

These next questions are what makes people the most uncomfortable. There is logic behind these questions. I have asked these questions numerous times with success. I would ask, do you have any guns, drugs, large amounts of cash, hand grenades, or dead bodies in the trunk? The typical response I would receive is a snicker or laugh. I did this questioning to break the ice a little bit with the driver. Of course he doesn't have hand grenades and dead bodies. At least I hope not! After the driver laughed, he would obviously say no. At this point I always circled back to the drugs. Ultimately, this is what I was looking to find out. I would individually ask the driver if he had any of the drugs. Any weed? Any heroin? Any meth? Any Crack? Any prescription pills? The reason behind these questions was to get a rhythm going with the answers. A person who does not have any of these items would easily and quickly answer no. The person who didn't have any of these items except one would easily and quickly answer no until they got to the one drug they actually had. When I would get to that specific drug, they would hesitate, repeat my question, or look directly at the area the drug was located. I would not only know that the driver had drugs on him, but I would be able to tell which drug and sometimes the location of the drug simply by the driver's response and reaction to that question. Obviously not everyone had drugs but a lot of times, drivers would confess or show indicators of possessing drugs when the officers had no suspicion of it.

If the person would easily and quickly answer the previous questions, I would ask one final question. I asked this question to simply get their reaction. Is there any problem with me searching your vehicle? I didn't even necessarily want to search their vehicle. I may not have had any probable cause to search their vehicle. But the response given tells a story to me.

Knowing the typical response and questioning of law enforcement can help ease your anxiety. Knowing what to expect and what could potentially happen is the best way to prepare. I'm not saying this will happen every time you get stopped but just that it can happen on occasion. No need to worry at all. If you are a good citizen and not breaking the law, then there is never any reason to worry or fear the police. Remember, we are actually the good guys.

Chapter 5

Do's and Don'ts

When officers pull you over for a traffic violation, it is their discretion whether or not to write you a citation. In my career, I have learned that most officers do not like writing tickets. I can't speak for every officer in this state. I can only speak through my own personal experience as an officer. It has been my experience that most people who have received tickets, have "talked" themselves into those tickets. What I mean by this is, the officer has pulled them over but has no intention of writing them a citation, only warning them. Once they get to the window, the driver is either rude, disrespectful, or argumentative towards the officer. Had they just been polite and respectful then more than likely they would have received a warning. So, I want to give you a list of Do's and Dont's to keep in mind if you're ever pulled over.

Do

Follow the recommendations in this book.

Be polite and respectful.

Answer questions honestly.

Notify officers of any weapons.

Don't

Fail to stop until you get to your driveway no matter how close you are. This happens so often and people believe that because they are home, officers have no authority to arrest, tow, or cite them. They feel they have made it to "Home Base" and they are free now. Not true!

Flee. No traffic offense or crime is worth putting others in danger and possibly killing someone by running from the police

Yell out the window and ask why you're being pulled over before the officer gets to the window. He will let you know after he determines the stop to be safe. Leaning and yelling out the window can seem aggressive and threatening to the officer.

Refuse to roll window down and just place documents against the window. This will result in possibly being placed under arrest.

Film on cell phone. Today's law enforcement officers are most likely filming the stop. By you filming , it becomes an unnecessary distraction to you and the officer.

Get out of vehicle unless instructed to do so. This can be seen as a threat or aggression to the officer.

Reach in areas the officer can't see or hide hands.

Argue about the reason for stop or why you are innocent. This should be done in the courtroom only! Not on the side of the road.

Name drop. Don't say, I know the chief, mayor, governor, etc. Most people don't know this but no chief, mayor, supervisor, governor, or anyone can require or order an officer to drop a citation. The only person that can dismiss a citation is the Judge, Prosecutor, or the officer that wrote it. Officers cannot be disciplined for issuing a legally justified citation. Telling their supervisors or boss will not help in getting your ticket dismissed.

Make rude comments like "I pay your salary," Why are you stopping me when there are drug dealers and murderers out there?" "Do you not have anything better to do?"

Speed off in anger after receiving the citation. I once had a vehicle sling mud and gravel on me when they spun the tires to leave. On another occasion I had stopped a vehicle for speeding, after receiving their citation they took off speeding and I clocked them even faster than I had originally wrote them for. Needless to say this will result in additional charges.

A lot of these listed items are not required by law. In fact, if you never say a word at all other than to identify yourself, then you aren't breaking any laws. I always like to tell people that the best way to conduct yourself is to simply be honest, polite, and respectful. You have a way better chance of getting a warning this way rather than acting irate, disrespectful, or argumentative. The entire situation will go so much smoother for you and the officer if you act in a mature and respectful manner.

Chapter 6

Your Rights-Your Requirements

Everything up to this point are my personal recommendations on how to conduct yourself when dealing with law enforcement. These important recommendations are the best way I know how to help your experience go as smooth as possible. It is equally important to know what your rights are and what your required to do on traffic stops.

Your Rights

Stop Location

If you ever feel unsafe in the location where the officer is trying to stop you, then you have the right to proceed to a safer location. The best way to let the officer know this is what you're doing is to follow the recommendation in Chapter 2 and use your blinker and begin to slow down. The best locations to pull over are well lit areas and gas stations, if available.

Remain Silent

You always have the right to remain silent. If you do not wish to communicate with the officer, then I would recommend that you inform the officer this rather than just sitting there speechless. It can be confusing to the officer whether or not there is a speech problem, hearing problem or otherwise. Try to keep in mind, officers deal with all walks of life so this is a possibility for the officer to think there is something wrong with you medically. Some have asked me, how do I let the officer know I want to remain silent and still be respectful about it? I would recommend that you tell the officer that you are not being uncooperative, you will gladly provide your documents but you respectfully wish to remain silent and not answer any questions.

Consent to Search

In order for any law enforcement officer to conduct a search of your vehicle they must have one of three things. They must have probable cause, a search warrant signed by a judge, or consent from the driver or owner. If an officer requests permission to search your vehicle, you have the right to refuse. If you decide to grant the officer permission, then you also have the right to be present during that search and you can, at any time, revoke that permission. For example, if you grant permission to search and the officers begin to search in the front of the vehicle, if you decide you don't want them to continue searching in the trunk, then you can stop them at that time. Keep in mind, if the officers find any evidence of a crime during any portion of the consensual search, they now have probable cause to finish the search. Also if a police K-9 has shown indication on your vehicle, this is considered probable cause for the officer to search without your permission.

Citation Instructions

If you receive a citation, you have a right to understand the instructions. If you do not understand how to take care of the citation, simply ask the officer to explain it. Typically, you will have one of two directions on the citation to fulfill the requirements. There will either be a phone number to call within a certain amount of time, or a court date and time to attend. Make sure you understand this so that you avoid your license being suspended. Normally, if there is a phone number that you're required to call then there will be a time frame you have to do this in. A lot of people get confused and think they have to have it paid within this time frame. It is only required that you call and make arrangements for the citation. If you are a new driver and under the age of 18, then some departments will notify your parents in the mail with your citation information.

Citation Signature

When you receive a citation, some departments will ask you to sign it. Some departments may hand you something like a receipt, and others will hand you a copy of the citation. You have the right to refuse to sign. If you do sign it, it is not an admission of guilt, only a promise to take care of the requirements of that citation. The law no longer requires your signature on a citation.

Court Dates

If you receive a citation and do not agree to the charges, then you have a right to contest it. As mentioned in the previous chapter, never argue with the officer on the side of the road. The time to argue is in court. This is your time to give your side of the story to the judge. This is your time to bring in any witnesses and evidence to support your case.

Law enforcement ID

Some departments have specialized units that patrol in non-typical vehicles, like vans or other regular vehicles with no markings. They will be wearing plain clothes as well. If you are stopped by one of these officers, I would recommend stopping in a safe location as discussed previously. You have a right to request identification from an officer who is not in a clearly marked uniform which displays his name, badge, and department patch.

Miranda Rights

You have the right to remain silent. Anything you say or do, can and will be used as evidence against you in the court of law. You have the right to speak with an attorney and have him or her present with you before and during any questioning. If you cannot afford an attorney, one will be appointed to represent with without cost and before any questioning. If you decide to answer questions now, without an attorney present, you still have the right to stop answering questions at any time. Officers will ask; Do you understand your rights? Having these rights in mind, do you wish to answer questions now without an attorney present?

Your Requirements

Pull Over
You are required to pull your vehicle over at the first available safe location. If you pass three gas stations and a Walmart

parking lot and continue driving, then it's reasonable for the officer to believe you aren't stopping and possibly hiding contraband, or planning an escape.

Identification

You are required to provide identification. If you don't have your identification card with you, then the officer will ask you for your name, date of birth, social, address and other vital information to properly identify you. Yes, you have the right to remain silent, but you are required to provide identifying information to the officer. Once you have provided this information, then you may remain silent.

Insurance/Registration

There are some citizens that believe that they do not have to have their vehicles registered and a valid license to drive. They believe that they are "traveling" and not driving. This is not true and you are, in fact, required to have your vehicle properly registered and insured at all times. Remember, driving a motor vehicle in this state is a privilege, not a right. In order to maintain that privilege, you must obey and follow the laws of the road. Not having insurance and registration will only set you up for criminal and civil liability.

Exit the Vehicle

If an officer requests you to step out of the vehicle, then you are required to do so. Law enforcement officers do this for safety and investigative reasons.

Rolling down Windows

We've all seen videos online where the driver of the vehicle refuses to roll down their window for the officer. They will put their identification against the window with a note that says they are exercising their right to remain silent. I can't speak for every state but I can say in this state, you are required to roll the window down when an officer tells you to.

Accepting Citations

It is your right to refuse to sign a citation. The law no longer requires a signature but it does require that you accept the citation from the officer. If you refuse to accept the citation, then the officer will have to place you under arrest and take you forthwith to the judge.

Citation Instructions

If you receive a citation, you are required to follow the instructions of that citation. It can either be calling within a certain amount of time, showing up to the court date provided, or setting up a court date. You can enter one of three different pleas; guilty, not guilty, or no contest. If you call and make arrangements to pay that citation, then that is a guilty plea. You can ask for a court date, enter a not guilty plea, and have a trial. This is where you will present your evidence and testimony about the case. The third option is you can enter a no contest plea which is no admission of guilt but you will pay the fine. No contest pleas, like guilty pleas, go on your record as a conviction.

Chapter 7

Worst Case Scenarios

As a driver, you're going to make mistakes. It's inevitable. Since this book is targeted towards the newer and younger drivers, I want to go over the worst case scenarios that you may face. The worst thing you could possibly do is take a simple mistake and make it worse by adding on to it. You're going to make mistakes in your life. No one is perfect and officers are aware of this.

Throughout my career I have been in multiple pursuits where the driver has fled from law enforcement because of something as small as their license were suspended. It is not worth putting your life and the lives of the public in danger for something as small as a suspension of your operators.

So let's take a look at a few examples of worst case scenarios in different situations.

You are a minor and you have beer in the car. Officers will confiscate the beer, call and release you to your parents, and send a "Juvenile Petition" to the courts for you to attend a court hearing at a later date. Vehicle will be towed or released to your parents.

You are a minor and you have drugs in the car. Officers will confiscate the drugs, call and release you to your parents, and send a "Juvenile Petition" to the courts for you to attend a court hearing at a later date. Vehicle will be towed or released to your parents.

You are a minor and you have been drinking. Officers will make sure you don't need medical attention. They will give you a field sobriety test to determine how intoxicated you are. Transport you back to the office for a breath test and paperwork. Officers will then release you to your parents and send a "Juvenile Petition" to the courts for you to attend a court hearing at a later date. The vehicle will be towed or released to your parents.

You are a minor and you've just ran away from home. Officers will contact your parents and release you to them.

You are a minor and you don't have a valid driver's license. Officers will contact your parents and release you and the vehicle to them. If no one can drive the vehicle, it will be towed to the wrecker lot.

You can see that everything listed above will result in you going home safe. These are just a few offenses that are possible with minors and new drivers. My point in writing this, is to show you the big picture before you get yourself in this situation. In my experience, people commit very minor traffic infractions and then make it worse by fleeing from the officers and causing a pursuit. During this pursuit, lives are in danger including the driver, the officers, and innocent civilians. Nothing listed above is bad enough to run from the police. These worst case scenarios can be dealt with and they really aren't anything major that can't be solved with a judge. You may get in some trouble but it's better than possibly losing your life in a major vehicle crash as you try to run. Unless you have committed murder or robbery of some kind, you will most likely be released into the custody of your guardians. If you did happen to commit a major crime, the worst thing that would happen is you would be immediately taken before a circuit court judge for them to make a decision. If you're ever faced with this predicament, never make it worse by running from law enforcement. It will only end badly.

Chapter 8

Top 10 Reason for being pulled over by Police

Knowing ahead of time the most common reasons officers pull you over can help you prepare and avoid the situation all together. I have personally compiled this list together based off of my own experience with traffic enforcement. While this is not the only reasons you can be pulled over, it is a good start to making sure you can avoid them. This can vary for every department and every officer.

Speeding/Reckless Driving. State Code: 17C-6-1/17C-5-3

Everyone speeds on occasion. Most of the time, people don't even know what the speed limit is, especially if they're not familiar with the area. Try and pay attention to those speed limit signs. A lot of people get new sports cars and they want to try it out. This gets a lot of people in trouble. They do "doughnuts" in parking lots or drag race down the interstate and it never fails, they get pulled over. As an officer, I unfortunately have seen the consequences of these actions. I have worked many vehicle crashes with fatalities as a result of drag racing. It's simply not worth it. Slow down!

Expired Registration. State Code: 17A-9-2

This is common because people don't pay their taxes. In order to get your registration up to date, you have to pay your personal property taxes, take the receipt for proof of payment, and then pay for your registration at the DMV or online.

Expired MVI. State Code: 17C-16-9

The most common reason I see why people have expired inspection stickers is because the cost of fixing their vehicle is just too much for them to afford. For example, if you have a cracked windshield your vehicle will fail inspection. You have to pay $400-$500 to fix the windshield and then go and get your vehicle inspected. One thing to remember is if your inspection sticker is only expired within 90 days and you receive a citation, as long as you get it inspected within the allotted timeframe, the citation will be dismissed.

Stop Sign/Stop Light. State Code: 17C-12-5/17C-3-4

Although stop lights are violated a lot, more often, stop signs are violated. Everyone has heard of the "slow and go." It can be easy to do when you're in a hurry but the dangers of this are high. When you develop a habit of "slow and go" then it becomes routine. One day your routine could easily turn into a major "T-Bone" crash.

Cell Phone Violations. State Code: 17C-14-15

This has become just as bad, if not worse, than a drunk driver on the road. I have worked countless crashes where someone couldn't wait to respond to a text. This has caused numerous fatalities that I have personally seen. If there is one law that you would probably not get a warning from an officer, I would guess it to be this one.

Seatbelt Violations. State Code: 17C-15-49

I have noticed that a lot of people don't follow this law because they feel that it's their choice. Without getting too political, I would just say that I have personally seen again and again how seatbelts can and will save your life in a crash. I have also seen where seatbelts have caused injuries during crashes but the odds of it saving your life, in my experience, are much higher.

Swerving/Crossing the center line. State Code: 17C-7-5

Officers focus on this a lot because it is common among drunk drivers to cross over into oncoming traffic. Although, more and more drivers are doing this because of cell phone usage.

Failure to Signal. State Code: 17C-8-8b

Another common trait of drunk drivers. This can cause crashes as well, including rear end collisions and intersection related crashes.

Defective equipment. State Code: 17C-15-1

This is an easy one for people to miss on their vehicles. Before you get in your vehicle as a new driver, you should always walk around your vehicle before leaving and confirm that all of your lights are properly working, especially if you don't want to get stopped.

Registration lights. State Code: 17C-15-1

I personally don't ever remember actually writing a citation for this offense but have stopped for it numerous times. It can be difficult to see the license plate without these lights illuminating at night and therefore should be working. If a suspect would commit a crime, then witnesses would have a hard time seeing the plate which could be crucial for the investigation.

As you can probably see by now, a majority of traffic enforcement is for the purposes of maintaining roadway safety while you drive. Driving can be a very dangerous game. It is not to be taken lightly when you're behind the wheel. As a new driver, it is important for you to develop good driving habits and obey the traffic laws. It is the intention of this book to show you what to expect during a traffic stop as well as developing good driving behaviors. Furthermore, how to avoid being pulled over at all. With good driving habits, you create safer roads for you and other drivers.

Chapter 9

Other Common Traffic Violations of New Drivers

In the previous chapter, I explained the most common reasons for being pulled over. In this chapter I'll go over other common violations that are popular among newer and younger drivers that cause them to get pulled over by police. We've all been young before and we've all made mistakes. Knowing these other common violations can give you a heads up before it happens and you can take steps in correcting or avoiding them all together.

Following too Closely. State Code Reference: 17C-7-10.

This is common among new and younger drivers because they haven't yet figure out how long it will take for their vehicle to come to a complete stop. According to the National Highway Traffic Safety Administration, if you are traveling at 55 miles per hour(mph), it will take you approximately 265 feet on dry payment to come to a complete stop. This is factoring in your "Driver reaction distance" and actual "braking distance." The typical reaction time to perceive a threat such as someone or something in the road is about ¾ of a second and then you have to factor in an additional ¾ of a second to decide to react to that threat for a total of 1.5 seconds which your vehicle has traveled 121 feet at 55 mph. Then you hit the brakes and it will take an additional 144 feet to stop. That is of course if the driver was paying attention when the threat of something in the roadway appeared and whether or not the pavement was dry. If the pavement was wet, then the vehicle would travel even further. Always maintain a safe distance from the vehicle in front of you while driving. Also, it is equally important to maintain a good distance when you're stopped in traffic behind a vehicle. Leave enough space to move out of the lane if necessary and also far enough back just in case you are hit from behind, so you don't get pushed into the vehicle in front of you.

Light Restrictions. State Code Reference: 17C-15-26.

Many people like to decorate their vehicles with special lighting of all kinds of different colors. I've seen green, blue, red, purple, etc. It is against the law to operate a vehicle on any highway with any color other than white or amber. I've seen several vehicles lately that have a blue in color "Uber" lighted sign in their front window while driving on the highway. I actually got confused for a minute because I couldn't figure out if it was an undercover officer or not. For this very reason, that is why this law is in affect. Any lighting of any color other than white or amber can only be operated while on private property. I know it looks cool, but this can result in you getting pulled over by law enforcement.

Loud Exhaust. State Code Reference: 17C-15-34.

Many drivers do not know about this law. A lot of newer and younger drivers love to personalize their vehicles when they get them. It's new and exciting to have your own ride. You get that new sports car or new "jacked up" truck and the first thing you want to hear is that power through that altered loud exhaust. Some people have diesel trucks and for whatever reason love to see it spit out that black smoke when they "rev" their engine or take off from a stop. You should know, that loud exhaust that puts out excessive smoke, is illegal and can cause you to get pulled over. That exhaust has to be manufacturers or equivalent.

Drag Racing. State Code Reference: 17C-6-8.

Imagine getting your license for the first time. You've maintained good grades just as your parents have wanted. You're one of the lucky ones and your parents buy you that brand new sports car you've always dreamed of having. Now you and your friends are out having fun for the first time alone without your parents. You decide to show off your new car to your friends as you pull up to a stop light next to another fast sports car. You make eye contact of the driver next to you and you both have the same challenging idea. You don't see any cops around, the road ahead is clear of other drivers, and its late at night. The light turns green and the race is on! I explain this little story because I've seen and heard this story a hundred different times from all kinds of new drivers. Unfortunately, I have also seen this story end tragically as well. In this scenario, you would be lucky if you get pulled over by police because that means it ended good. That officer has potentially saved your life. When you're a new or younger driver, you don't think about how one dog, one kid, one lane-change of an innocent driver, or one piece of road debris can cause you to lose control, flip your car and potentially kill yourself or others. I have seen this same scenario take the lives of innocent kids and it's my hope that you will take this lesson to heart and avoid it all together. It's such a preventable scenario yet so many younger newer drivers feel they are invincible. This is simply not true. It can very likely happen to you.

Obviously, there are several traffic violations that you can be pulled over for but I wanted to cover the most common among the newest drivers of the roadway. The key here is to be prepared for what can happen if you violate any of these laws. If you take each of these law into consideration before you get behind the wheel and do everything you can to prevent, prepare, and avoid them, then the chances of you getting pulled over by police are greatly reduced.

Chapter 10

Most Common Excuses Drivers Give Officers

Up until now, I hope I have provided enough information for you to understand and deal with everything involved in a police traffic stop. You have been supplied with the applicable laws, knowledge of your rights and requirements, what is expected of you as well as what to expect from the officers. Knowledge of this should help in making the encounter smoother, less stressful, and safer for everyone.

Now I would like to provide you with the top excuses that are given to officers when they pull you over. I want you to have an understanding that the officer stopping you has heard these a thousand times before. More than likely, if you give these excuses, it will have no effect on the officer's decision to write you a citation or not because most of these excuses are not excuses at all. They are just statements to support the officer's decision to charge you. You can talk to your friends, parents, teachers, neighbors, or anyone else that you know that has been pulled over by police and I can almost guarantee you that they have provided at least one of these excuses during the stop. It's my hope that if you get pulled over by police, that you don't provide these excuses. They simply, don't work. Just for fun, ask your parents if they've given one of these.

Speeding Violations

"I wasn't paying attention."

I wanted to start with this excuse because it is probably the one that is given most often. Officers can understand this and it is the most believable. It is easy to get distracted by school, work, kids, parents, sporting events and friends. Although it doesn't help you to get out of a ticket, officers can respect the fact that you were honest enough to state the truth.

"I am late/in a hurry."

Everyone is late when they're going to work, school, or event. The officer will more than likely just tell you to leave earlier next time. Being late for school is not an excuse to speed through the school zone and endanger other kids.

"I was just going with the flow of traffic."

This one is used quite often. Here's the thing, you may be right in that you were going with the flow of traffic. The officer may have clocked you and the vehicles in front of you for speeding. Unfortunately, the officer stopping you is only one officer. He can't stop every car and you may be the one he gets to first. Just because ten cars in front of you were speeding, doesn't excuse the speed you were doing.

"I'm not from the area."

There are speed limit signs on most roadways across the nation. The only thing this excuse tells the officer is that you weren't looking and obeying the traffic signs on the road.

"I have to use the bathroom/I'm sick."

This could be a good excuse. We've all had an emergency once or twice in our lives. Unfortunately, this is used so often to law enforcement that it is no longer believed. A lot of times, when I have heard this excuse from a driver, we have passed several public places that have restrooms inside before I stopped the vehicle. So knowing that a driver has passed several bathrooms to speed through town just to use their own, isn't an excuse.

"I don't know the speed limit."

This one is along the same lines as "I'm not from the area." It only tells the officer that the driver wasn't paying attention to the roadway signs. It also supports the officer's testimony in court if you decide to contest the ticket and say you weren't speeding as the officer states. How can the judge believe you if you didn't even know the speed limit?

"My cruise control was set."

This is used often on major highways. Drivers like to set their cruise controls, or at least say they set their cruise controls, and then let the officer know this. The officer will completely ignore this excuse. Officers use calibrated speed measuring devices that are checked for accuracy before and after each speed enforcement detail they work. They are required to do this for courtroom testimony. More than likely the GPS or app being utilized by the driver are not calibrated and I believe most of them give a warning to this effect.

"I didn't see you there."

So as long as you don't see an officer, this means you can speed? Definitely not a good excuse. This tells the officer that you have a habit of speeding as long as an officer is not around.

"I have an emergency."

When you're on an airplane, the flight attendants will explain the oxygen masks should be placed on yourself first and then you should help other passengers. The reason for this, is you are of no help to anyone else if you get hurt or injured yourself. In the same way, if there is an emergency that you are trying to get to, speeding down the highway placing yourself in danger isn't going to do you any good. If there is an emergency in the vehicle with you at the time of stop, then the officer is going to contact the paramedics.

"My kids were distracting me."

This is understandable as a lot of police officers are mothers and fathers as well. The best option in this case is to pull over and handle the situation on the side of the road. Driving faster down the road puts you and your kids lives in danger.

Stop Light Violations

"It was yellow, not red."

The yellow lights are there to prepare you well ahead of time to slow down and stop. A lot of people see the yellow light as a starter gun going off at a track field. They see the yellow light and slam on the gas to get through it so they don't have to wait another minute. This has caused a countless number of wrecks throughout my career.

"I was just following the car in front of me."

This goes along with the speeding excuse of "I was just going with the flow of traffic." I will say again, just because the person in front of you ran through the red light doesn't give you an excuse to run through the same light.

"My brakes aren't working properly."

This is probably the worst excuse you can give. Officers are obligated to maintain the safety of the roadway. If you tell the officer that your brakes aren't working, then they have no choice but to tow your vehicle for safety reasons. Most of the time, when drivers give me this excuse and I explain that I have to tow their vehicle, they simply confess they lied. That's the quickest way to receive a citation!

Expired Registration/Expired Inspection sticker.

"I was going to do that today."

This response reminds me of the drunk drivers I arrest. The number one answer we get from drunk drivers when we ask them how much they have had to drink is "one beer." Usually when this excuse is given for expired registrations, the officer will give the driver a citation. I personally allow them to go and get the registration as they have stated they were going to do and then bring in proof that they actually got it done on that day, then I dismiss it. As long as it wasn't expired too long. This is a good way for the officer to determine whether or not the driver was telling the truth. This is also a great way to make the driver get it fixed if they weren't telling the truth.

"My husband/wife is responsible for that."

It's amazing how many husbands and wives get "thrown under the bus" by their spouses when getting pulled over by police for registration stickers and inspection stickers. Even though this is entertaining to the officer, it's still not a good excuse.

"I can't afford it."

In order to get your registration for your vehicle, you must pay your personal property taxes. Unfortunately, "Uncle Sam" isn't very forgiving. I've mentioned this already, driving is a privilege, not a right. We all have to pay our taxes.

Cell phone violations

"I was just scratching my face."

This law can be very entertaining to law enforcement because of the actions of drivers when they are on their phones and pass one of us. I've see them have their phones up to their face talking and when they see us they will literally drop their phones and never move their hand from their face. I always wonder how badly they damage their phone from dropping it. They will pretend to scratch their face as if I didn't see the phone in their hand before they dropped it.

"I was just holding it, I had it on speaker."

The key here is "hands free." Most vehicles now have Bluetooth. Try and remember to use it!

"I was switching songs."

Is it really worth getting in a wreck over finding the right song?

These are just the most common excuses law enforcement hears on traffic stops but there have been a lot more as well. Some people get very creative in their excuses to traffic violations. The best thing you can do is just be honest when you make a mistake. Be real with the officer and don't try and give excuses and insult the officer's intelligence. More than likely, the officer who has stopped you has already heard the excuse you are about to give. Just accept responsibility, follow the recommendations in this book and everything will go a lot smoother.

Closing

After stopping thousands of vehicles in my career, I have
noticed a common misunderstanding among the newer driver.
They simply don't know what to do or what to expect. The
drivers will do some of the wildest things when responding to
blue lights in their rearview mirror. They have wrecked,
continued driving to their house, stopped in the middle of the
highways, and completely froze up in fear. When talking to
these same drivers, they don't know what to do, what to say, or
what documents the officers are wanting. I've come to a
conclusion that it's not their fault. It's the fault of our system
not teaching them properly. We prepare them for everything
about operating a motor vehicle except what to do when they
encounter law enforcement.

In today's society, there is a lot of negative media about law
enforcement through news outlets and social media. It has
created a certain level of fear and rebellion towards law
enforcement. It is my hope in this book to provide a real
perspective through the eyes of a police officer on how to
respond to traffic stops. I want the reader to understand
reasoning behind officer's actions. I want the reader to know
how they can respond to help the process to go smoother. I
believe that problems on traffic stops stem from a simple

misunderstanding and miscommunication. With the
information that you have learned, you are now equipment with
the knowledge of exactly what to expect and how to respond to
getting pulled over by police.

You can be acknowledged in my next Book!

Is there a topic about law enforcement that you would like to know more about?

Do you have questions or want advise from law enforcement on a specific topic?

Have you ever wondered how Police do certain things?

Just reach out to me personally and let me know your thoughts, questions, or suggestions for my next book!

MyPoliceBooks@gmail.com

References

West Virginia State Code

National Highway Traffic Safety Administration

West Virginia Police Officers

STAY SAFE AND THANK YOU FOR READING!

CPSIA information can be obtained
at www.ICGtesting.com
Printed in the USA
LVHW050416160321
681656LV00022B/720

9 781715 583750